SCHOLASTIC

English

Made Simple

Ages 5–6

Revision & Practice

Year 1
P2

Build knowledge and confidence in English

SCHOLASTIC

First published in the UK by Scholastic, 2025

Scholastic Education, Bosworth Avenue, Warwick, CV34 6UQ

Scholastic Ireland, 89E Lagan Road, Dublin Industrial Estate, Glasnevin, Dublin, D11 HP5F

1 2 3 4 5 6 7 8 9   5 6 7 8 9 0 1 2 3 4

A CIP catalogue record for this book is available from the British Library.

ISBN 978-0702-33661-4

Printed and bound by Leo Paper Products Ltd, China.

The book is made of materials from well-managed, FSC®-certified forests and other controlled sources.

MIX Paper | Supporting responsible forestry FSC® C020056

www.scholastic.co.uk

For safety or quality concerns:
UK: www.scholastic.co.uk/productinformation
EU: www.scholastic.ie/productinformation

Author
Catherine Casey

Editorial team
Rachel Morgan, Audrey Stokes, Christine Bruce, Julia Roberts, David & Jackie Link

Design team
Andrea Lewis, QBS Learning

Illustrations
Cover (dragon & pencil) Tigatelu/iStock; (books) the8monkey/iStock

Robot: VIGE.CO/Shutterstock

QBS Learning: p26, p28 (flowers), p29, p34 (wink), p44 (bus), p50, p51 (house), p55, p56, (flowers)

Other: p6 (rainbow) Tartila/Shutterstock; p7, 18 (zebra) d3verro/Shutterstock; p7, 15 (pizza) lawang design/Shutterstock; p8 (worm) VikiVector/iStock; p8 (nose) Maman Suryaman/Shutterstock; p9 (cactus) Elena Istomina/Shutterstock; p10 (rain cloud) Studio_G/Shutterstock; p10 (roller boots) Softachka/Shutterstock; p10 (tortoise) Simply Amazing/Shutterstock; p11 (snowman) Only _up/ Shutterstock; p11 (broccoli) Magicleaf/Shutterstock; p11 (puzzle piece) sewonboy/Shutterstock; p12 (milkshake) aelitta/iStock; p13 (grasshopper) Nsit/Shutterstock; p13 (puddle) Sylfida/Shutterstock; p14, 25, 46 (sunflower) Dernkadel/Shutterstock; p14 (fox) d3verro/Shutterstock; p14 (plums) Andrii Bezvershenko/Shutterstock; p14 (snail) WinWin artlab/Shutterstock; p15, 24, 54 (owl) GoodStudio/Shutterstock; p15, 40 (frog) d3verro/Shutterstock; p15 (pterodactyl) lanrward/Shutterstock; p15 (laptop) johavel/Shutterstock; p20 (sloth) Maquiladora/Shutterstock; p16, 52 (train) Tomacco/Shutterstock; p17 (sweets) Texturis/Shutterstock; p17 (lion) d3verro/Shutterstock; p17 (rocket) vivat/Shutterstock; p17 (hippo) d3verro/Shutterstock; p18, 23 (moon and stars) Begimail/Shutterstock; p18, 24 (girl jumping) Colorfuel Studio/Shutterstock; p19 (cheetah) d3verro/Shutterstock; p19 (dog) Good Studio/Shutterstock; p19, 40 (elephant) d3verro/Shutterstock; p20 (corn) Andrii Bezvershenko/ Shutterstock; p20 (dinosaur & nest) Teguh Mujiono/Shutterstock; p20 (eggs) Mihai Gruianu/Shutterstock; p21 (bread) Neliakott/Shutterstock; p21 (snowman) Panda Vectors/Shutterstock; p21 (carrot) Andy.Illustrator/Shutterstock; p25, 44, 46 (football) Kanate/Shutterstock; p22, 48 (cats) ayutaka/iStock; p23 (hats) Tartila/Shutterstock; p23 (tractor) Tanislava/Shutterstock; p23 (trees) vivat/Shutterstock; p23 (socks) RZN_desing/Shutterstock; p23, 54 (cupcakes) yuwnis07/Shutterstock; p23, 48 (boxes) olesia_g/Shutterstock; p23 (lamp) Kolonko/Shutterstock; p23 (paintbrushes) Dmytro K/Shutterstock; p23 (watches) StockSmartStart/Shutterstock; p23 (dresses) YummyBuum/ Shutterstock; p24 (dishes) olly2polly/Shutterstock; p24 (tennis racket & ball) Handatko/Shutterstock; p25 (window) pikepicture/Shutterstock; p25 (door) Oxy_gen/Shutterstock; p25 (music notes) Kharom Pleedee/iStock; p28 (bird) spirkaart/Shutterstock; p28 (kitten) KoAlia_draws/Shutterstock; p28 (mouse) Mvshop/Shutterstock; p30, 34 (shoes) KutuzovaDesign/Shutterstock; p30 (paper) sumkinn/Shutterstock; p34 (boys) Tana-mame/iStock; p31 (zip) A 5/ Shutterstock; p33 (clapping emojis) Sudowoodo/Shutterstock; p34, 42, 48 (paint splodge) Neliakott/Shutterstock; p34, 35 (woman thinking) mentalmind/ Shutterstock; p34, 35 (sink) Fancy Tapis/Shutterstock; p34, 35 (glass of water) Frogella/Shutterstock; p34, 35 (linked chains) Nadia Snopek/Shutterstock; p34 (shaking hands) Lerinalnk/Shutterstock; p34, 35 (sinking boat) BlueRingMedia/ Shutterstock; p34 (empty glass) Frogella/Shutterstock; p34, 35 (water tank) MaryValery/Shutterstock; p34, 35 (bank) Eloku/Shutterstock; p34 (horn) VectorPlotnikoff/Shutterstock; p36 (sandwich) LadadikArt/iStock; p36 (orange juice carton) shock77/iStock; p36 (dog with ball) YG Studio/Shutterstock; p36 (sign) Sensvector/Shutterstock; p36, 37 (chick & egg hatching) ivector/ Shutterstock; p38 (van) Golden Sikorka/Shutterstock; p38 (vet) denayunebgt/ Shutterstock; p38 (vest) johavel/Shutterstock; p39 (glove) Look_Studio/ Shutterstock; p39 (olive) lemono/iStock; p39 (heart) Graphics Studio MH. We offer you the best things/iStock; p39 (dove) elenabs/iStock; p40 (fish) d3verro/Shutterstock; p40 (fairy) Natalllenka.m/Shutterstock; p40 (feet) Julee Ashmead/Shutterstock; p40 (dolphin) d3verro/Shutterstock; p40 (alphabet) andreysharonov/Shutterstock; p40 (sphere) Sensvector/Shutterstock; p40 (mobile phone) Carkhe/Shutterstock; p40 (trophy) CleanVector/Shutterstock; p42, 48 (yak) d3verro/Shutterstock; p42, 48 (yoghurt) Shany Muchnik/ Shutterstock; p42, 43 (cherry)FoxGrafy/Shutterstock; p42, 43, 53 (bunny) mentalmind/Shutterstock; p42, 43 (woman) tynyuk/Shutterstock; p42, 43 (dog) Macrovector/Shutterstock; p42, 43 (celebration emoji) Tally18/Shutterstock; p42, 43 (berry) Ksenia Gromova/Shutterstock; p42, 43 (family) Tenstudio/ Shutterstock; p44 (apples) Alody/Shutterstock; p46 (toothbrush) Anatolir/ Shutterstock; p46 (snowball) MaryValery/Shutterstock; p46 (popcorn) Kumeko/ Shutterstock; p46 (eyebrow) ivector/Shutterstock; p46 (ball) sabelskaya/ iStock; p46 (hairbrush) lemono/iStock; p46 (flower) TheArtist/iStock; p46 (foot) Easy_Company/iStock; p46 (tooth) Jane_Kelly/iStock; p46 (sun) Davyd Kopych/ iStock; p47 (raindrop) Net Vector/Shutterstock; p47 (snowflake) graficriver_ icons_logo/Shutterstock; p47 (blueberries) Ksenia Gromova/Shutterstock; p47 (doormat) StockSmartStart/Shutterstock; p48 (cot) Quang Vinh Tran/ Shutterstock; p48 (man) tynyuk/Shutterstock; p52 (girl) Galkin_K/iStock; p51 (robot) Nursery Art Design/Shutterstock; p51 (whale) d3verro/Shutterstock; p51 (snake) d3verro/Shutterstock; p53 (toy truck) SurfsUp/Shutterstock; p54 (magnifying glass) chuhastock/Shutterstock; p54 (boy) seamartini/iStock; p57 (slide) Bobrik74/Shutterstock

Contents

How to use

This book has been written to help children reinforce the English skills they have learned in school. It is divided into sections covering a range of topics from the National Curriculum. Use it little and often to practise skills and increase confidence. You can choose to work through each section in order or focus on specific topics. At the back of the book is a **Progress tracker** to enable you to record what has been practised and achieved.

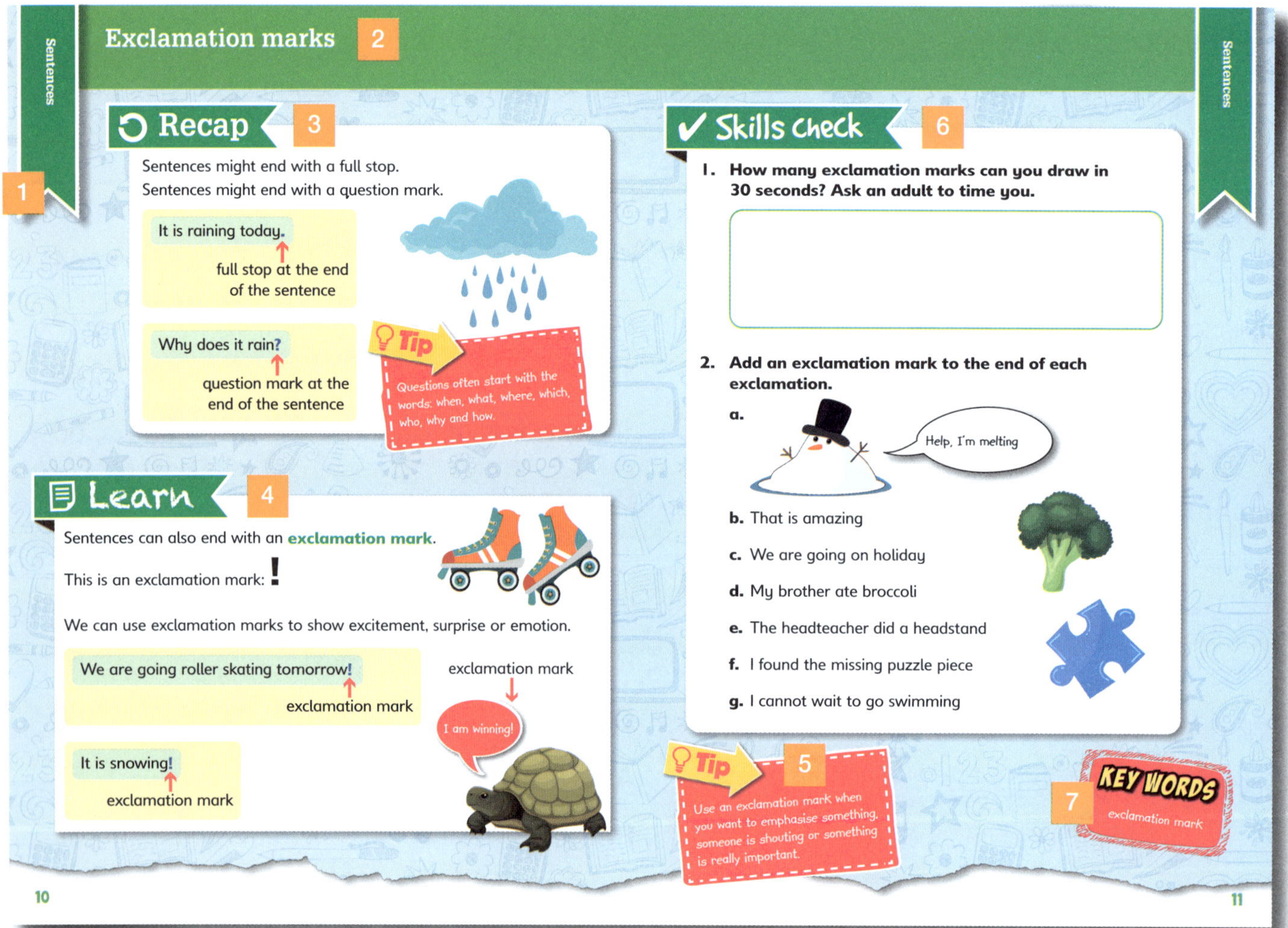

1. Chapter title
2. Topic title
3. Each page starts with a **recap** summarising what the children should know.
4. In the **learn** section there are clear explanations and examples, using illustrations and diagrams, where relevant.
5. **Tips** provide short and simple advice to aid understanding.
6. The **skills check** sections enable children to practise what they have learned with answers at the back of the book.
7. **Key words** that children need to know are displayed. Definitions for these words can be found in the **Glossary**.

Tips for using this book at home

Using this book, alongside the English being done at school, can boost children's mastery of the concepts. Be sure not to get ahead of schoolwork or to confuse your child.

Keep sessions to an absolute maximum of 30 minutes. Even if children want to keep going, short amounts of focused study on a regular basis will help to sustain learning and enthusiasm in the long run.

Word lists These are the words you need to learn to spell.

Year 1

the	his	go	ask
a	has	so	friend
do	I	by	school
to	you	my	put
today	your	here	push
of	they	there	pull
said	be	where	full
says	he	love	house
are	me	come	our
were	she	some	
was	we	one	
is	no	once	

Capital letters and full stops

Recap

A **sentence** is a group of words that make sense.

Learn

Sentences start with a **capital letter** and end with a **full stop**.

Capital letters	A	B	C	D	E	F	G	H	I	J	K	L	M
Lower-case letters	a	b	c	d	e	f	g	h	i	j	k	l	m

Capital letters	N	O	P	Q	R	S	T	U	V	W	X	Y	Z
Lower-case letters	n	o	p	q	r	s	t	u	v	w	x	y	z

A full stop shows the reader the sentence has ended.

Tip

A full stop is a small dot.

● ✓ ఠ ✗ ○ ✗

capital letter at the beginning of the sentence

I like playing football**.**

full stop at the end of the sentence

capital letter at the beginning of the sentence

There is a rainbow in the sky**.**

full stop at the end of the sentence

KEY WORDS

sentence
capital letter
full stop

✓ Skills Check

1. Circle the capital letters.

A a N e E g r Q

d G D B b R i M

2. Draw lines to match the capital letters to the lower-case letters.

n c g h j t

J T N C H G

3. Add a full stop to the end of each sentence.

a. The sun is shining

b. I went to the park on Saturday

c. I have a pet zebra and a whale lives in my bath

4. Rewrite each sentence with a capital letter at the beginning and a full stop at the end.

a. we had pizza for lunch

____

b. my coat is red

____

c. the teacher told us a joke

____

Question marks

Recap

A sentence begins with a capital letter and ends with a full stop.

Learn

When we ask something, it is called a question.

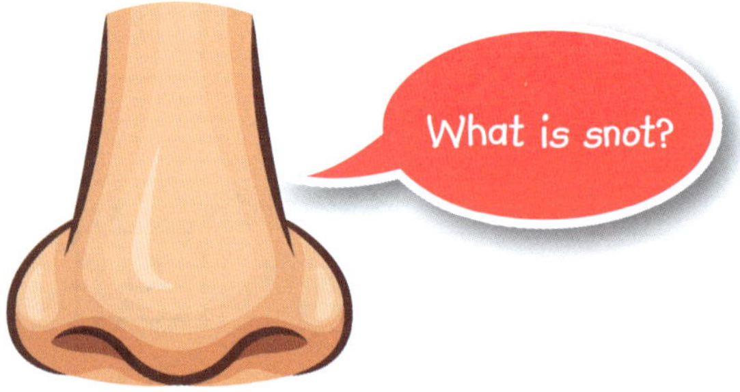

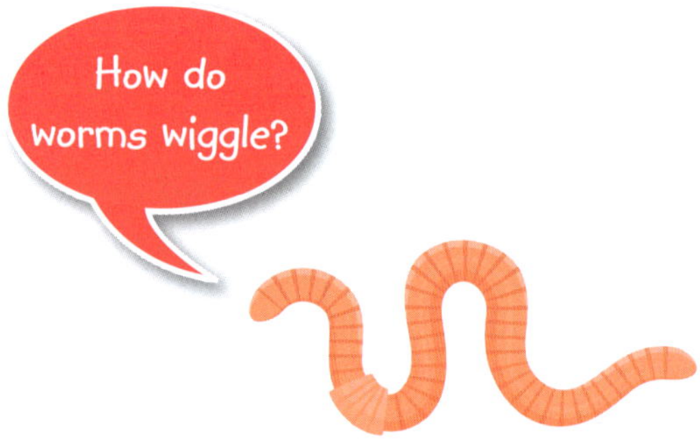

When we write a question down, we end with a **question mark**.

Here is a question mark: **?**

Why do people have different coloured eyes?

↑ question mark at the end of the sentence

What colour is a giraffe's tongue?

↑ question mark at the end of the sentence

KEY WORDS

question mark

✓ Skills Check

1. Draw a line of question marks.

? ? ? ____

2. Which of these are questions? Tick them.

I like chocolate ice cream. ☐

Can an elephant run? ☐

My favourite animal is an elephant. ☐

How do you make ice cream? ☐

3. Add a question mark to the end of each question.

a. Why is a cactus prickly

b. Did dinosaurs have feathers

c. How many stripes does a zebra have

4. Write your own question. Remember to start with a capital letter and end with a question mark.

____

____

____

Tip

Here are some question words you can use to ask a question:

how where what when why which who

Exclamation marks

Recap

Sentences might end with a full stop.
Sentences might end with a question mark.

It is raining today.
↑
full stop at the end of the sentence

Why does it rain?
↑
question mark at the end of the sentence

Tip

Questions often start with the words: when, what, where, which, who, why and how.

Learn

Sentences can also end with an **exclamation mark**.

This is an exclamation mark: **!**

We can use exclamation marks to show excitement, surprise or emotion.

We are going roller skating tomorrow!
↑
exclamation mark

It is snowing!
↑
exclamation mark

exclamation mark
↓

✓ Skills Check

1. How many exclamation marks can you draw in 30 seconds? Ask an adult to time you.

2. Add an exclamation mark to the end of each exclamation.

a.

b. That is amazing

c. We are going on holiday

d. My brother ate broccoli

e. The headteacher did a headstand

f. I found the missing puzzle piece

g. I cannot wait to go swimming

Tip

Use an exclamation mark when you want to emphasise something, someone is shouting or something is really important.

KEY WORDS

exclamation mark

Capital letters for names and 'I'

Recap

Here is the alphabet. The capital letters are in bold.

Capital letters	**A**	**B**	**C**	**D**	**E**	**F**	**G**	**H**	**I**	**J**	**K**	**L**	**M**
Lower-case letters	a	b	c	d	e	f	g	h	i	j	k	l	m

Capital letters	**N**	**O**	**P**	**Q**	**R**	**S**	**T**	**U**	**V**	**W**	**X**	**Y**	**Z**
Lower-case letters	n	o	p	q	r	s	t	u	v	w	x	y	z

We use capital letters at the beginning of a sentence.

Learn

We use capital letters for people's names.

Alec **M**aya **B**en **M**ax **E**lla **A**mira **M**r **G**reen **M**rs **J**ackson

We use a capital letter for the word **I**.

capital letter ↓

I like milkshake. ✔

i like milkshake. ✘

capital letter ↓

I am a superhero. ✔

i am a superhero. ✘

✔ Skills Check

1. Write the letters of the alphabet as capital letters.

Capital letters							

Capital letters							

Capital letters							

Capital letters					

2. Circle the words that should start with a capital.

a. ava went to the park.

b. mr green was a teacher.

c. Yesterday, max made a cake.

d. The lady who lives next door is called mrs jackson.

e. ben went to the park with jun.

f. alec and tom had ice cream after lunch.

3. Rewrite each sentence with the correct capital letters.

a. i like hopping like a grasshopper.

____

____

b. When it started raining, i splashed in the puddles.

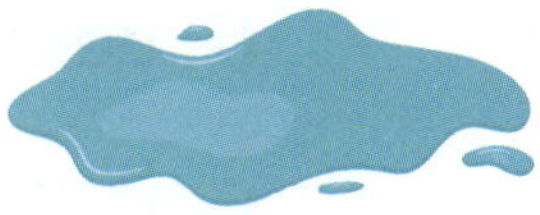

____

____

____

Tip

We use capital letters for names, the word I and at the beginning of a sentence.

Spaces between words

Recap

A sentence is a group of words that makes sense.

Learn

We put a small space between words when we are writing. This helps the reader to read the words more easily.

Igrewasunflower. ✗
I grew a sunflower. ✓
I   grew   a   sunflower. ✗

✓ Skills Check

1. Read these sentences aloud. Clap between each word.

a. Foxes hunt at night.

b. Bees make honey.

c. Plums are purple.

2. Draw a line between the words in each sentence. The first one has been done for you.

a. I | had | an | apple | after | lunch.

b. Giraffes have blue tongues.

c. The snail slithered down the path.

3. Copy the sentences. Remember to put a space between the words.

a. Owls have big eyes.

____

____

b. There was a frog in the pond.

____

____

c. Some dinosaurs flew.

____

____

4. Ava wrote a sentence. She forgot to put spaces between the words.

Ilikepizza.

a. Draw lines between the words to show where the spaces should be.

b. Copy the sentence, remembering the spaces between the words.

____

Tip

Put a lollipop stick, a piece of dried pasta, a pom pom or your finger after each word to practise leaving spaces.

When you are typing a sentence, you use the spacebar between words.

Sequencing words

Recap

A sentence is a group of words that makes sense.

When we write, we put a small space between each word.

small gaps between words

Sloths move slowly.

sentence

Learn

Sentences are made up from a group of words. The words must be in the right order to make sense.

train. on the I went ✗

I went on the train. ✓

Tip Say the sentence aloud to check it makes sense.

✓ Skills Check

1. Rearrange the words to make a sentence.

a. sweets. I like

____

b. roared lion The loudly.

____

c. space. rocket into went The

____

____

d. mud. hippo in rolled The

____

____

2. Are the words in the correct order?
Put a tick for yes and a cross for no.

a. sky. stars the shining are in The ☐

b. Ben rode his bike at the park. ☐

c. Cheetahs have spots. ☐

d. legs. have Snakes do not ☐

Using 'and'

Recap

Joining words join two words or two groups of words together. We can use the word **and** to join words together.

fish **and** chips

salt **and** pepper

girls **and** boys

the moon **and** stars

Learn

A sentence is a group of words that make sense.
We can use the word **and** to join sentences.

Zebras have stripes. Leopards have spots.

Zebras have stripes **and** leopards have spots.

I washed my face. I cleaned my teeth.

I washed my face **and** I cleaned my teeth.

Ava jumped in the puddles. Max danced in the rain.

Ava jumped in the puddles **and** Max danced in the rain.

✔ Skills Check

1. Write the word 'and' to join the sentences together.

a. My bike is blue __________ Tom's bike is red.

b. Pia is playing with the bricks __________ Jun is reading a book.

c. Sam had an apple __________ Sasha had a banana.

2. Join the sentences together using 'and'.

a. Cheetah are fast. Sloths are slow.

____

____

b. Dogs bark. Cats purr.

____

c. Elephants live on land.
Whales live in the sea

____

____

Tip

Remember to remove the full stop and change the capital letter of the second sentence (unless it's a name or I).

KEY WORDS

joining words

Sequencing sentences

Recap

We order words to make sure a sentence makes sense.

corn. farmer The grows

The farmer grows corn.

Learn

You can put sentences in order to make a story.
A story has a beginning, a middle and an end.

beginning	The dinosaur built a nest.
middle	The dinosaur laid an egg in the nest.
end	The egg hatched.

✓ Skills Check

1. Number the sentences to put them in the correct order. The first one has been done for you.

a. The dinosaur built a nest. ___1___

The egg hatched. ___3___

The dinosaur laid an egg in the nest. ___2___

b. Then she baked fresh bread. __________

The baker sold the fresh bread. __________

The baker got up early to bake. __________

c. It had snowed. __________

The boy put a hat and a scarf on his snowman. __________

The boy built a snowman. __________

d. The gardener planted some seeds. __________

The carrots grew. __________

The gardener ate the carrots. __________

e. She kicked the ball. __________

She scored a goal. __________

Ella put on her football boots. __________

Adding 's' or 'es'

Say some words that begin with the letter **s**.

Recap

What sound does the letter **s** make?

Learn

A **suffix** is a letter or group of letters you add to the end of a word to change its meaning.

We add **s** or **es** to words to make them **plural**.

Singular means there is only one.

cat

Plural means there is more than one.

cats

For most words, we add **s**.

cat + **s** = cat**s**

toy + **s** = toy**s**

frog + **s** = frog**s**

door + **s** = door**s**

car + **s** = car**s**

If a word ends in **x**, **z**, **sh**, **ch** or **ss**, we add **es**.

fox + **es** = fox**es**

buzz + **es** = buzz**es**

dish + **es** = dish**es**

watch + **es** = watch**es**

dress + **es** = dress**es**

KEY WORDS

suffix

plural

singular

✓ Skills Check

1. Add 's' to make these words plural.

a. hat______ 

b. tractor______ 

c. tree______ 

d. sock______ 

e. cake______ 

f. star______ 

2. Add 'es' to make these words plural.

a. box_______ 

b. wish_______ 

c. watch_______ 

d. brush_______ 

e. dress_______ 

Tip

Look at the end of the word to decide if it needs an *s* or *es* to make it plural.

Adding 'ing'

Recap

A suffix is a letter or group of letters you add to the end of a word to change the meaning.

owl + **s** = owls

dish + **es** = dishes

Learn

We can add the suffix **ing** to words.

jump + **ing** = jumping

I jump in puddles.

I am jumping in puddles.

cook + **ing** = cooking

I cook lunch.

I am cooking lunch.

draw + **ing** = drawing

I can draw a cat.

I am drawing a cat.

play + **ing** = playing

I play tennis.

I am playing tennis.

✓ Skills Check

1. Add the suffix 'ing' to these words.

a. look + ing = ____________________

b. paint + ing = ____________________

c. help + ing = ____________________

d. sing + ing = ____________________

e. grow + ing = ____________________

2. Choose the correct word to complete each sentence.

a. look | looking

I ____________________ out of the window.

I am ____________________ out of the window.

b. paint | painting

He is ____________________ the door.

He can ____________________ doors.

c. help | helping

I am ____________________ my mum to wash the car.

I ____________________ Gran cook the dinner.

d. sing | singing

I can ____________________.

I like ____________________.

e. grow | growing

Flowers ____________________ in the garden.

We are ____________________ sunflowers.

Tip

Say the sentence aloud to check it makes sense.

Adding 'ed'

Recap

A suffix is a letter or group of letters you add to the end of a word to change the meaning.
s, **es** and **ing** are suffixes.

Learn

We can add the suffix **ed** to some words to change it into the **past tense**.

Tip

Something in the past tense has already happened.

walk + **ed** = walked

I walk up the hill.
I walked up the hill.

play + **ed** = played

I play tennis.
I played tennis.

wash + **ed**

I wash the dishes.
I washed the dishes.

✔ Skills Check

1. Colour in the suffix 'ed' in these words.

a.	w	a	l	k	e	d
b.	p	l	a	y	e	d
c.	h	e	l	p	e	d
d.	l	o	o	k	e	d
e.	j	u	m	p	e	d
f.	c	o	o	k	e	d
g.	w	a	s	h	e	d
h.	p	u	l	l	e	d

2. Add the suffix 'ed' to these words.

a. smash________

b. bang________

c. push________

d. pick________

e. clean________

f. thump________

g. crash________

h. wish________

i. buzz________

KEY WORDS

past tense

Adding 'er' and 'est'

Recap

Suffixes are a letter or group of letters. Suffixes are added to the end of a word to change its meaning.

Learn

We can add the suffixes **er** and **est** to some words.

tall

tall + **er** = taller

tall + **est** = tallest

The red flower is the tallest.

The yellow flower is the shortest.

The yellow flower is tall.

The orange flower is taller.

The red flower is the tallest.

small

small + **er** = smaller

small + **est** = smallest

The kitten is small.

The bird is smaller.

The mouse is the smallest.

✔ Skills Check

1. Colour in the suffix for each word.

a.

s	m	a	l	l	e	r

s	m	a	l	l	e	s	t

b.

l	o	n	g	e	r

l	o	n	g	e	s	t

c.

o	l	d	e	r

o	l	d	e	s	t

d.

n	e	w	e	r

n	e	w	e	s	t

2. Add the suffix to these words.

a. short + er = ______________________

short + est = ______________________

b. high + er = ______________________

high + est = ______________________

3. Circle the tallest building.

Tip

We use **er** to compare two things. We use **est** to compare three or more things.

Adding the prefix 'un'

Recap

When you add a **prefix** to a word its meaning changes.

Learn

A prefix is a letter or group of letters you add to the start of a word to change its meaning.

un is a prefix.

When **un** is added to a word the new word means the opposite.

happy  unhappy  unhappy means **not** happy

tie  untie  untie means **not** tied

fold  unfold  unfold means **not** folded

kind  unkind  unkind means **not** kind

✓ Skills Check

1. Add the prefix 'un' to these words.

a. ________happy

b. ________tie

c. ________do

d. ________block

e. ________fold

f. ________cover

g. ________zip

h. ________kind

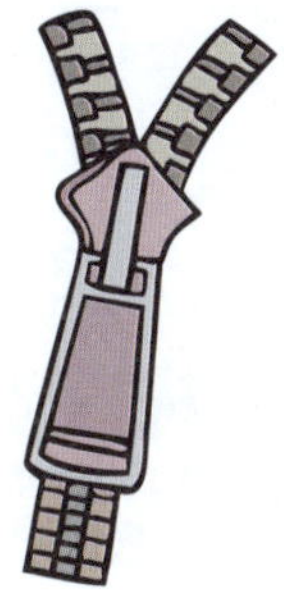

2. Can you find the words with the prefix 'un' in the wordsearch?

uncover | untie | unfold | undo | unzip

u	n	c	o	v	e	r	n	v	w
h	l	p	w	q	u	s	a	c	v
c	b	n	a	y	t	u	t	u	l
u	n	t	i	e	u	n	l	n	b
t	i	o	q	j	o	f	l	d	p
d	c	b	n	n	b	o	l	o	b
u	n	z	i	p	n	l	t	r	w
q	w	r	t	y	u	d	g	h	j

Tip

Prefixes are added to the start of a word. Suffixes are added to the end of a word.

KEY WORDS

prefix

Days of the week

Recap

There are seven days in a week.

The days of the week always start with a **capital letter**.

Learn

Here are the days of the week:

Monday, **Tuesday**, **Wednesday**, **Thursday**, **Friday**, **Saturday**, **Sunday**

Skills Check

1. Can you find the days of the week in the wordsearch?

Monday Tuesday Wednesday Thursday
Friday Saturday Sunday

M	M	O	N	D	A	Y	Y	T	C
D	A	R	T	M	O	N	Y	U	S
T	H	U	R	S	D	A	Y	E	A
T	L	V	K	B	S	N	N	S	T
M	S	U	N	D	A	Y	Y	D	U
W	N	O	M	R	Y	V	B	A	R
W	E	D	N	E	S	D	A	Y	D
E	R	T	Y	G	H	C	A	T	A
D	R	F	R	I	D	A	Y	P	Y

2. Copy the days of the week.

Monday ____________________

Tuesday ____________________

Wednesday ____________________

Thursday ____________________

Friday ____________________

Saturday ____________________

Sunday ____________________

KEY WORDS

capital letters

3. Fill in the missing letters.

M	o	n		a	y			
T		e	s	d	a	y		
W	e	d	n	e	s			
		u	r	s	d	a	y	
			d	a	y			
S	a	t			d	a	y	
			d	a	y			

4. Clap the days of the week.

Mon/day

Tues/day

Wednes/day

Thurs/day

Fri/day

Sat/ur/day

Sun/day

Tip

Breaking the words up into chunks can help you remember how to spell them.

'nk' words

Recap

We can sound out words to help us read them.

p i nk   th i nk   b a nk

Learn

nk

Here are some words with the **nk** sound.
Have a go at saying the words aloud.

pink		thank	
think		sank	
sink		drank	
drink		tank	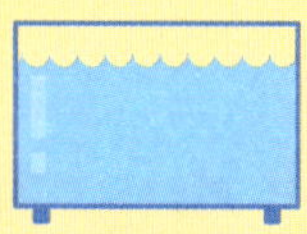
link		bank	
wink		honk	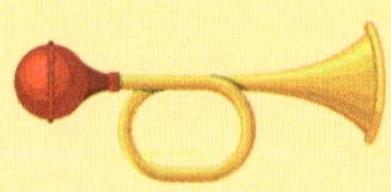

✓ Skills Check

1. Add the missing letters to complete these words.

a.  thi________

b.  li________

c. 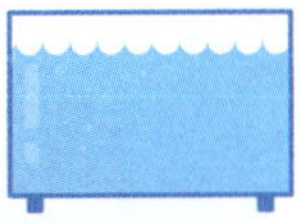 ta________

d. 

ba________

2. Add the missing letters to complete these words.

a. The boat s________________ to the bottom of the sea.

b. My shoes are p________________.

c. Can I have a d________________ please?

d. Wash your hands at the s________________.

The 'ch' sound

Recap

We can **segment** words to spell them.
We can **blend** words to read them.

l u n ch
lunch

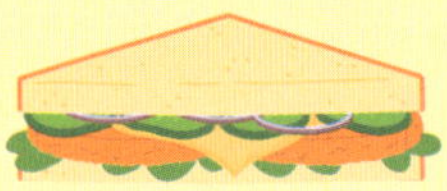

Learn

ch

r i ch	rich
m u ch	much
ch i ck	chick
ch i n	chin

tch

h u tch	hutch
c a tch	catch
d i tch	ditch
p a tch	patch

Let's look at words with the ch sound. This sound can be spelled ch or tch.

Have a go at segmenting and blending the words.

Read the sentences. Can you find the words with the **ch** sound?

Can the dog fetch the ball?

We are cooking in the kitchen.

It was such a wonderful day.

Which way is it to the park, please?

✓ Skills Check

1. Colour in the ch sound in each word.

a. | h | a | t | c | h |

b. | c | h | i | p |

c. | l | a | t | c | h |

d. | c | h | e | s | t |

e. | s | n | a | t | c | h |

f. | i | t | c | h |

2. Circle the correct spelling for each word.

a.	match	mach
b.	bench	bentch
c.	cruntch	crunch
d.	pitch	pich
e.	churtch	church
f.	pinch	pintch

Tip

When you split the words into their sounds it is called segmenting. When you blend the sounds together to read a word, it is called blending.

KEY WORDS

segmenting
blending

Words ending in the 'v' sound

Recap

van

vet

vest

Learn

Words that end in the **v** sound are spelled with a **v** and an **e**.

v → **ve**

thieve	massive	carve	solve	leave
halve	serve	shove	prove	halve

✔ Skills Check

1. Can you find the words that end with the v sound?

h	d	s	t	b	c	v	w
a	n	l	p	j	h	t	r
v	r	e	a	b	o	v	e
e	t	e	k	w	r	t	n
n	w	v	n	v	v	c	r
l	t	e	m	g	i	v	e
m	o	v	e	k	l	n	m
p	d	t	v	a	l	v	e

have
sleeve
give

move
above
valve

2. Circle the words that are spelled correctly.

shelve	shelv	curve	starve	starv
activ	active	massive	nerv	weave
weav	curv	nerve	move	massiv

3. Add the missing letters to complete these words.

a. glo________

b. oli________

c. lo________

d. do________

‘ph’ words

Recap

fish

feet

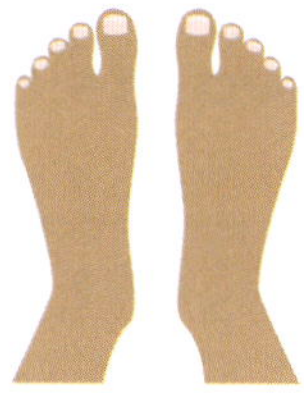

fairy

frog

Learn

ph makes the same sound as **f**

dolphin

alphabet

sphere

phone

elephant

trophy

✓ Skills Check

1. Colour in the ph sounds in the words.

a.

d	o	l	p	h	i	n

b.

s	p	h	e	r	e

c.

e	l	e	p	h	a	n	t

d.

p	h	o	n	e

e.

t	r	o	p	h	y

f.

a	l	p	h	a	b	e	t

2. Sort the words into the correct box.

dolphin	fairy	feet	trophy	phone
frog	fun	first	alphabet	sphere

f	ph
______________	______________
______________	______________
______________	______________
______________	______________
______________	______________

Words ending in 'y'

Recap

Read the words beginning with y.

yak

yellow

yoghurt

Learn

y at the end of a word makes an **ee** sound.

happy 

cherry 

bunny 

lady 

puppy 

party 

berry 

family 

✓ Skills Check

1. Add the y to the end of each word.

a. happ____

b. cherr____

c. bunn____

d. lad____

e. pupp____

f. part____

g. berr____

h. famil____

2. Circle the words that are spelled correctly.

happee lady bunny puppe parte

berry happy famile family bunee

3. Find the words that end in y.

happy
lady
cherry

h	a	p	p	y	n	y	c
g	f	g	h	w	r	t	h
w	r	t	h	l	n	m	e
w	c	v	k	a	e	r	r
r	s	b	v	d	l	l	r
b	e	r	r	y	p	p	y
t	b	p	a	r	t	y	g
f	a	m	i	l	y	n	v

family
party
berry

Contractions

Recap

We use a capital letter for the word **I**.

I like apples. How will **I** get to the park?
Ben and **I** played football.

Learn

This is called an **apostrophe**. ’

It shows a letter or letters are missing.

Sometimes we use apostrophes to shorten words.
These words are called **contractions**.

I’ll = I will
I’m = I am
I’ve = I have
I’d = I would
we’ll = we will
we’ve = we have

✓ Skills Check

1. Draw a line to match each word to the correct contraction.

I would	we'll
I am	I'm
I will	I've
we will	we've
we have	I'll
I have	I'd

2. Circle the contractions in these sentences.

a. I'm going to sing a song on the stage.

b. I've got a brother.

c. We'll have to walk to school.

d. We've got half an hour until the next bus.

e. I'll wait for you.

f. I'd like a drink.

KEY WORDS

apostrophe

contraction

Compound words

Recap

Read these words.

sun 

foot 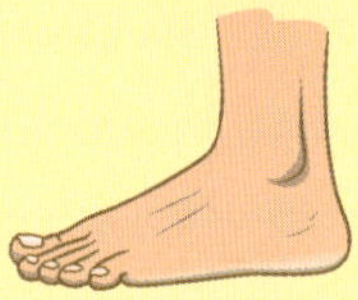

tooth 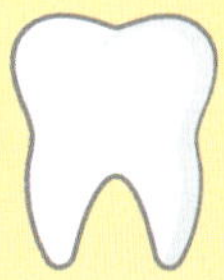

flower 

ball 

brush 

Learn

You can add two words together to make a new word.

tooth + brush = toothbrush 

snow + ball = snowball

sun + flower = sunflower 

foot + ball = football 

pop + corn = popcorn 

eye + brow = eyebrow 

Tip

Compound words are made from two other words joined together.

✓ Skills Check

1. Draw a line to join two words together and make a new word.

tooth	corn
snow	berry
sun	man
pop	shine
straw	paste

2. Add another word to create a compound word. Use the words in the box to match each picture.

flake   drop   berry   mat

a. rain_________________________

b. snow_________________________

c. blue_________________________

d. door_________________________

KEY WORDS

compound word

Tricky words (1)

Recap

What sounds do these letters make?

pet

ten

red

cot

box

sob

yak

yoghurt

yell

Learn

Some spellings don't follow the rules!

Have a go at reading and spelling these words:

In these words the y makes an igh sound.

by my

In these words the e makes an ee sound.

be he she we

In these words the o makes an oa sound.

go so no

✓ Skills Check

1. Write a line of each word.

a. be ______________________________

b. he ______________________________

c. she ______________________________

d. we ______________________________

e. go ______________________________

f. so ______________________________

g. no ______________________________

h. by ______________________________

i. my ______________________________

2. Choose a word from Question 1. How many times can you write it in 30 seconds? Ask an adult to time you.

Tip

Practise writing these words in fun ways. Can you write them in chalk? Can you make them out of modelling dough? Can you create them using letter magnets? How big can you write each word? How small can you write each word?

Tricky words (2)

Recap

Some words don't follow spelling rules.

Learn

Here are some more words that don't follow the rules!

the	today	said
are	was	you
there	where	one
school	house	some

Skills Check

1. Find the words in the wordsearch.

the
today
said
are
was
you

s	s	o	m	e	t	h	w
c	a	t	o	d	a	y	a
h	r	k	l	h	g	d	s
o	e	s	a	i	d	w	r
o	h	o	u	s	e	y	b
l	n	o	n	e	h	o	t
m	t	h	e	r	e	u	h
w	h	e	r	e	p	n	e

there
where
one
school
house
some

2. Copy these words.

a. the ______________________

b. today ______________________

c. said ______________________

d. are ______________________

e. was ______________________

f. you ______________________

g. there ______________________

h. where ______________________

i. one ______________________

j. school ______________________

k. house ______________________

3. Fill in the missing words. Use the words in the box.

said	house	One	was

Max lives in the ______________________ with a red door.

______________________ day a robot came to school.

There ______________________ a robot on the playground.

"I can see a robot," ______________________ Max.

Tip

Try making up a saying using the letters of a word to help you remember how to spell the word. For example:

was: whales are super!

said: snakes are impressive dancers!

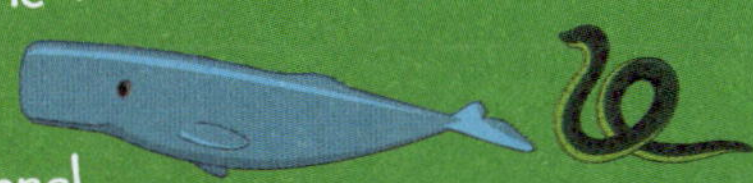

Titles, characters and events

Recap

A **sentence** is a group of words that makes sense.

Learn

Titles are headings that tell you what the piece of writing is about or what a story is called.

Characters are the people or animals in a story.

Events are things that happen in a story or report.

The Train Ride ← title

characters: Sam and Ella

Sam and Ella sat on the train, excitedly watching out the window. Suddenly, the train stopped.

events: sat on the train; watching out the window; the train stopped.

✓ Skills Check

1. Read the text. Answer the questions.

A Visit to the Vets

Pia and her nan were going to the vets.
Pia's bunny needed a check-up.
But the bunny did not want to get in the box.

a. What is the title?

____

b. Who are the two characters?

____

____

c. What are the three events?

____

____

____

____

____

____

**2. Read the text. Circle the title.
Underline the characters. Talk about the events.**

At the Park

Dad took Max to the park. Max
played in the sandpit with his truck.

KEY WORDS

characters
events
sentences
titles

Inference

Recap

We can find facts in a text.

The owl had white feathers and big yellow eyes.

Learn

We read text for meaning.
Sometimes the answers are in the text:

The cupcake lay on the floor at the boy's feet. Bits of mud and grass were stuck to the pink icing on the cupcake. Tears dripped down the boy's face.

Sometimes we can work out what has happened even when it doesn't say directly in the text, by looking for clues.

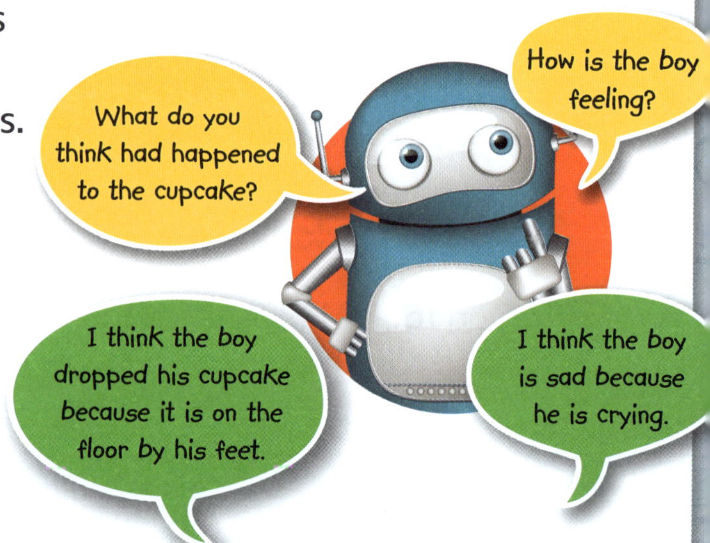

✓ Skills Check

Read the text and answer the questions.
Tick the correct answers.

Sam and his grandad were going fishing. Excitedly, Sam helped his grandad put the fishing rods in the car. "Can you get my fishing chair out of the shed?" asked Grandad. Sam looked for the chair in the shed. He saw a spider so he screamed and ran back to the car.

1. Where are Sam and his grandad going?

swimming ☐

fishing ☐

running ☐

2. Where was Grandad's chair?

in the kitchen ☐

in the car ☐

in the shed ☐

3. How did Sam feel about spiders?

scared ☐

excited ☐

happy ☐

Tip

When we look for clues in the text to answer questions, it is called **inference**. We infer something from the text.

KEY WORDS

inference

Predict what happens next

Recap

Predict means to guess what happens next.

Learn

We can use clues in a story to predict what might happen next.

Pia left her bike on the floor while she got an ice cream. The ice cream was big and it was a little bit wobbly. Pia saw her friend, Fred, and waved to him but she was not looking where she was going.

Here are the clues:

Pia left her bike on the floor → This tells us there is something to trip over.

The ice cream was big and wobbly. → This tells us the ice cream can fall easily.

Pia was not looking where she was going. → This tells us Pia will not see the bike.

✓ Skills Check

Read the text.

The New Slide

Ben went to the park. Ben liked the swings best. He did not like being high up or going fast. Today, there was a new slide at the park. The new slide was very high and fast. Ben went up all the steps to the new slide very slowly. When he got to the top, he looked down. It was a very long way – Ben was not very happy.

1. What do you think happened next? Tick your answer.

Ben does not want to go down the slide. ☐

Ben likes the slide because it is fast. ☐

Ben likes the slide because it is high. ☐

2. Explain why you chose the answer you did.

____

____

____

Tip

Look for all the clues as you read the text. Highlight the clues to help you.

KEY WORDS

predict

Glossary

A

apostrophes look like this **'** and can be used to show missing letters in a word.

B

blending is when we join the sounds together to read a word.

C

capital letters are A, B, C, D, E, F, G, H, I, J, K, L, M, N, O, P, Q, R, S, T, U, V, W, X, Y and Z.

characters are the people or animals in a story.

compound words are words made from two or more shorter words. Some compound words are toothpaste and sunshine.

contractions are shortened words, where an apostrophe is used to replace missing letters. Contractions include I'll and we've.

E

events are the things that happen in a story.

exclamation marks look like this **!** and are punctuation marks. Exclamation marks are used at the end of a sentence to emphasise something, to show shock or surprise, or when someone is shouting.

F

full stops look like this **.** and are punctuation marks. We use full stops at the end of a sentence.

I

inference is when we use clues to work something out when it is not explicit in the text.

J

joining words join two words or groups of words together. Joining words include and.

P

past tense tells us that something has already happened.

plural means more than one.

predict means to guess what will happen before it happens.

prefix is a letter or group of letters that is added to the start of a word to change the meaning.

Q

question marks look like this **?** and are punctuation marks used at the end of a question or when you are asking something.

S

segmenting is when we split a word up into its sounds to help us spell the word.

sentences are groups of words that make sense.

singular means there is only one.

suffix is a letter or group of letters added to the end of a word to change its meaning.

T

titles are how we name a piece of writing. A text might have a heading like How cars work. A story might have a name like The Yellow Balloon.

Answers

SENTENCES

Page 7

1 (A) a (N) e (E) g r (Q)
d (G) (D) (B) b (R) i (M)

2
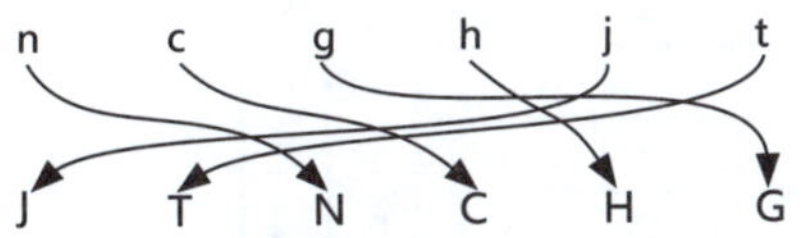

3 **a.** The sun is shining**.**
b. I went to the park on Saturday**.**
c. I have a pet zebra and a whale lives in my bath**.**

4 **a. W**e had pizza for lunch.
b. My coat is red.
c. The teacher told us a joke.

Page 9

2 I like chocolate ice cream. ☐
Can an elephant run? ☑
My favourite animal is an elephant. ☐
How do you make ice cream? ☑

3 **a.** Why is a cactus pricky**?**
b. Did dinosaurs have feathers**?**
c. How many stripes does a zebra have**?**

4 Accept any question written which starts with a capital letter and ends with a question mark.

Page 11

2 **a.** Help, I'm melting**!**
b. That is amazing**!**
c. We are going on holiday**!**
d. My brother ate broccoli**!**
e. The headteacher did a headstand**!**
f. I found the missing puzzle piece**!**
g. I cannot wait to go swimming**!**

Pages 12–13

1

Capital letters	**A**	**B**	**C**	**D**	**E**	**F**	**G**
Capital letters	**H**	**I**	**J**	**K**	**L**	**M**	**N**
Capital letters	**O**	**P**	**Q**	**R**	**S**	**T**	**U**
Capital letters	**V**	**W**	**X**	**Y**	**Z**		

2 **a.** (Ava) went to the park.
b. (Mr) (Green) was a teacher.
c. Yesterday, (Max) made a cake.
d. The lady who lives next door is called (Mrs) (Jackson.)
e. (Ben) went to the park with (Jun.)
f. (Alec) and (Tom) had ice cream after lunch.

3 **a. I** like hopping like a grasshopper.
b. When it started raining, **I** splashed in the puddles.

Pages 14–15

1 **a.** Foxes hunt at night. = 3 claps
b. Bees make honey. = 2 claps
c. Plums are purple. = 2 claps

2 **b.** Giraffes | have | blue | tongues.
c. The | snail | slithered | down | the | path.

3 **a.** Owls have big eyes.
b. There was a frog in the pond.
c. Some dinosaurs fly.

4 **a.** I|like|pizza.
b. I like pizza.

Page 17

1 **a.** I like sweets.
b. The lion roared loudly.
c. The rocket went into space.
d. The hippo rolled in mud.

2 **a.** sky. stars the shining are in The ☒
b. Ben rode his bike at the park. ☑
c. Cheetahs have spots. ☑
d. legs. have Snakes do not ☒

Page 19

1 **a.** My bike is blue **and** Tom's bike is red.
b. Pia is playing with the bricks **and** Jun is reading a book.
c. Sam had an apple **and** Sasha had a banana.

2 **a.** Cheetah are fast **and** sloths are slow.
b. Dogs bark **and** cats purr.
c. Elephants live on land **and** whales live in the sea.

Page 21

1 **b.** Then she baked fresh bread. **2**
The baker sold the fresh bread. **3**
The baker got up early to bake. **1**
c. It had snowed. **1**
The boy put a hat and a scarf on his snowman. **3**
The boy built a snowman. **2**
d. The gardener planted some seeds. **1**
The carrots grew. **2**
The gardener ate the carrots. **3**
e. She kicked the ball. **2**
She scored a goal. **3**
Ella put on her football boots. **1**

VOCABULARY

Page 23

1 **a** hat**s**
b. tractor**s**
c. tree**s**
d. sock**s**
e. cake**s**
f. star**s**

2 **a.** box**es**
b. wish**es**
c. watch**es**
d. brush**es**
e. dress**es**

Page 25

1
a. look**ing**
b. paint**ing**
c. help**ing**
d. sing**ing**
e. grow**ing**

2
a. I **look** out of the window.
I am **looking** out of the window.
b. He is **painting** the door.
He can **paint** doors.
c. I am **helping** my mum to wash the car.
I **help** Gran cook the dinner.
d. I can **sing**.
I like **singing**.
e. Flowers **grow** in the garden.
We are **growing** sunflowers.

Page 27

1

a.	w	a	l	k	e	d
b.	p	l	a	y	e	d
c.	h	e	l	p	e	d
d.	l	o	o	k	e	d
e.	j	u	m	p	e	d
f.	c	o	o	k	e	d
g.	w	a	s	h	e	d
h.	p	u	l	l	e	d

2
a. smash**ed**
b. bang**ed**
c. push**ed**
d. pick**ed**
e. clean**ed**
f. thump**ed**
g. crash**ed**
h. wish**ed**
i. buzz**ed**

Page 29

1

a.	s	m	a	l	l	e	r	
	s	m	a	l	l	e	s	t
b.	l	o	n	g	e	r		
	l	o	n	g	e	s	t	
c.	o	l	d	e	r			
	o	l	d	e	s	t		
d.	n	e	w	e	r			
	n	e	w	e	s	t		

2
a. short**er**
short**est**
b. high**er**
high**est**

3

Page 31

1
a. unhappy
b. untie
c. undo
d. unblock
e. unfold
f. uncover
g. unzip
h. unkind

2

u	n	c	o	v	e	r	n	v	w
h	l	p	w	q	u	s	a	c	v
c	b	n	a	y	t	u	t	u	L
u	n	t	i	e	u	n	l	n	b
t	i	o	q	j	o	f	l	d	p
d	c	b	n	n	b	o	l	o	b
u	n	z	i	p	n	l	t	r	w
q	w	r	t	y	u	d	g	h	j

SPELLING

Page 32–33

1

M	M	O	N	D	A	Y	Y	T	C
D	A	R	T	M	O	N	Y	U	S
T	H	U	R	S	D	A	Y	E	A
T	L	V	K	B	S	N	N	S	T
M	S	U	N	D	A	Y	Y	D	U
W	N	O	M	R	Y	V	B	A	R
W	E	D	N	E	S	D	A	Y	D
E	R	T	Y	G	H	C	A	T	A
D	R	F	R	I	D	A	Y	P	Y

2 Monday, Tuesday, Wednesday, Thursday, Friday, Saturday, Sunday

3

M	o	n	**d**	a	y			
T	**u**	e	s	d	a	y		
W	e	d	n	e	s	**d**	**a**	**y**
T	**h**	u	r	s	d	a	y	
F	**r**	**i**	d	a	y			
S	a	t	**u**	**r**	d	a	y	
S	**u**	**n**	d	a	y			

Page 35

1
a. thi**nk**
b. li**nk**
c. ta**nk**
d. ba**nk**

2
a. s**ank**
b. p**ink**
c. d**rink**
d. s**ink**

Page 37

1

a.	h	a	t	c	h	
b.	c	h	i	p		
c.	l	a	t	c	h	
d.	c	h	e	s	t	
e.	s	n	a	t	c	h
f.	i	t	c	h		

2
a. (match) mach
b. (bench) bentch
c. cruntch (crunch)
d. (pitch) pich
e. churtch (church)
f. (pinch) pintch

Page 39

1

h	d	s	t	b	c	v	w
a	n	l	p	j	h	t	r
v	r	e	a	b	o	v	e
e	t	e	k	w	r	t	n
n	w	v	n	v	v	c	r
l	t	e	m	g	i	v	e
m	o	v	e	k	l	n	m
p	d	t	v	a	l	v	e

2 (shelve) shelv (curve) (starve) starv

activ (active) (massive) nerv (weave)

weav curv (nerve) (move) massiv

3
a. glo**ve**
b. oli**ve**
c. lo**ve**
d. do**ve**

Page 41

1

a. d o l p h i n

b. s p h e r e

c. e l e p h a n t

d. p h o n e

e. t r o p h y

f. a l p h a b e t

2

f	ph
fairy	dolphin
feet	trophy
frog	phone
fun	alphabet
first	sphere

Page 43

1
a. happ**y**
b. cherr**y**
c. bunn**y**
d. lad**y**
e. pupp**y**
f. part**y**
g. berr**y**
h. famil**y**

2 happee (lady) (bunny) puppe parte

(berry) (happy) famile (family) bunee

3

h	a	p	p	y	n	y	c
g	f	g	h	w	r	t	h
w	r	t	h	l	n	m	e
w	c	v	k	a	e	r	r
r	s	b	v	d	l	l	r
b	e	r	r	y	p	p	y
t	b	p	a	r	t	y	g
f	a	m	i	l	y	n	v

Page 45

1
I would → I'd
I am → I'm
I will → I'll
we will → we'll
we have → we've
I have → I've

2
a. (I'm) going to sing a song on the stage.
b. (I've) got a brother.
c. (We'll) have to walk to school.
d. (We've) got half an hour until the next bus.
e. (I'll) wait for you.
f. (I'd) like a drink.

Page 47

1
tooth → paste
snow → man
sun → shine
pop → corn
straw → berry

2
a. rain**drop**
b. snow**flake**
c. blue**berry**
d. door**mat**

Page 50–51

1

s	s	o	m	e	t	h	w
c	a	t	o	d	a	y	a
h	r	k	l	h	g	d	s
o	e	s	a	i	d	w	r
o	h	o	u	s	e	y	b
l	n	o	n	e	h	o	t
m	t	h	e	r	e	u	h
w	h	e	r	e	p	n	e

3 Max lives in the **house** with a red door.
One day a robot came to school.
There **was** a robot on the playground.
"I can see a robot," **said** Max.

READING

Page 53

1
a. A Visit to the Vets
b. Pia and Nan
c. Going to the vets, needing a check-up, not getting in the box.

2 (At the Park)
<u>Dad</u> and <u>Max</u>

Page 55

1 swimming ☐ fishing ☑ running ☐
2 in the kitchen ☐ in the car ☐ in the shed ☑
3 scared ☑ excited ☐ happy ☐

Page 57

1 Ben does not want to go down the slide. ☑
Ben likes the slide because it is fast. ☐
Ben likes the slide because it is high. ☐

2 Example explanation: I think Ben does not want to go down the slide because it is very high and fast. Ben is not happy when he looks down. He goes up the steps slowly. Ben does not like going fast or being high up.

Progress tracker

Sentences

Practised	Achieved		
❐	❐	Capital letters and full stops	6
❐	❐	Question marks	8
❐	❐	Exclamation marks	10
❐	❐	Capital letters for names and 'I'	12
❐	❐	Spaces between words	14
❐	❐	Sequencing words	16
❐	❐	Using 'and'	18
❐	❐	Sequencing sentences	20

Vocabulary

Practised	Achieved		
❐	❐	Adding 's' or 'es'	22
❐	❐	Adding 'ing'	24
❐	❐	Adding 'ed'	26
❐	❐	Adding 'er' and 'est'	28
❐	❐	Adding the prefix 'un'	30

Spelling

Practised	Achieved		
❐	❐	Days of the week	32
❐	❐	'nk' words	34
❐	❐	The 'ch' sound	36
❐	❐	Words ending in the 'v' sound	38
❐	❐	'ph' words	40
❐	❐	Words ending in 'y'	42
❐	❐	Contractions	44
❐	❐	Compound words	46
❐	❐	Tricky words (1)	48
❐	❐	Tricky words (2)	50

Reading

Practised	Achieved		
❐	❐	Titles, characters and events	52
❐	❐	Inference	54
❐	❐	Predict what happens next	56

Notes